Therapy Animals

BY CONNIE COLWELL MILLER

amicus high interest

Amicus High Interest is an imprint of Amicus
P.O. Box 227, Mankato, MN 56002
www.amicuspublishing.us

Library of Congress Cataloging-in-Publication Data
Miller, Connie Colwell, 1976-
Therapy animals / by Connie Colwell Miller.
pages cm -- (Animals with jobs)
Summary: "Describes what therapy animals do, where they work, how they are trained, and which kinds of animals are best for certain jobs. Includes stories about real animals who have provided therapy to people"-- Provided by publisher.
Includes index.
ISBN 978-1-60753-381-8 (library binding) -- ISBN 978-1-60753-429-7 (ebook)
1. Animals--Therapeutic use--Juvenile literature. 2. Animals as aids for people with disabilities--Juvenile literature. I. Title.
RM931.A65M55 2014
615.8'5158--dc23
2013001424

Editor Wendy Dieker
Series Designer Kathleen Petelinsek
Page production Red Line Editorial, Inc.

Photo Credits
Carol Guzy/The Washington Post/Getty Images, cover; Jose Luis Stephens/Alamy, 4; iStockphoto/Thinkstock, 7, 8, 19; Shutterstock Images, 11; MCT/Getty Images, 12; Dennis Sabo/Shutterstock Images, 15; Denis Kuvaev/Shutterstock Images, 16; Art Directors & TRIP/Alamy, 20; Hemera/Thinkstock, 23; Boston Globe/Getty Images, 24; Spencer Grant/Getty Images, 27; Joe Drivas/Getty Images, 28

Table of Contents

Therapy Animals 5

Animals That Heal 10

Learning the Job 14

People Partners 21

Amazing Animals 25

Glossary 30

Read More 31

Websites 31

Index 32

Therapy dogs can help people get stronger or healthier.

Therapy Animals

Murphy is an animal with a job. She works as a **therapy** dog. Murphy helps kids like Megan. Megan has **cerebral palsy**.

Megan is learning to walk. But she has never taken a step. Today, Megan wants to give Murphy a treat. Megan's **therapist** stands the girl in a **walker**. She points to Murphy. "Give Murphy this treat."

Megan takes a step toward Murphy. Wow! Then, Murphy takes a step backward. Megan takes another step forward. And Murphy takes another step backward.

Megan takes a few more steps. Finally, Megan gets tired. She stops. Murphy sits down. Megan gives Murphy the treat. Megan smiles. She did it! With help from Murphy, Megan took her first steps.

Q Why did Murphy step backward?

Good therapy dogs can help kids work hard to get stronger.

A Murphy was pushing Megan to work harder. Good therapy dogs know how to help people work hard.

Therapy animals like Murphy work in hospitals and nursing homes. The people these dogs help might be sick or have **disabilities**. Others have hurt a part of their body. Some are getting better after an operation.

Therapy is hard work. Sometimes people don't want to keep trying. Therapy animals help these people keep working hard.

Learning to ride a horse can help people with some disabilities.

Animals That Heal

Therapy animals must be friendly and calm. They cannot be afraid of people or hospital machines. Dogs must not jump on people, bark, or growl. Other therapy animals must not nip, scratch, or shy away from people. They shouldn't hurt or frighten the people they are trying to help.

Friendly dogs can make people happy and calm.

Swimming with dolphins can be good therapy for some people.

Q How do horses work in therapy?

Almost any type of animal can be a therapy animal. Most are dogs like Murphy. Horses can also have this job. A cat might live at a nursing home. Rabbits, guinea pigs, and even birds can help people. Some people even work with dolphins! The most important thing is that the animal likes to be around people.

A Horses help children with **autism**. The rhythm of how the horse moves helps them. These children work on developing physical and social skills.

Learning the Job

Most animals need training to work in therapy. The amount of training they need depends on the work they do. Some animals just visit people to cheer them up. Basic **obedience** training might be enough for dogs who do this work. Animals such as cats and rabbits usually are not trained. They just need to be good with people.

This therapy dog cheers up people in nursing homes.

Therapy dogs need to be trained well. They listen to their handlers.

Q Is there a school for therapy dogs who need lots of training?

Most therapy animals are dogs with lots of training. They need to learn to support people the way Murphy does. Therapy dogs train hard for this work. They practice responding to their **handlers**' commands. They might be told to jump on a hospital bed or to run next to a child. Therapy dogs need to learn to act quickly.

A A group called Pet Partners holds training classes for dogs. They make sure the dogs will do a good job.

Therapy animals must be healthy and clean. They go to the vet to make sure they are not sick. Sick animals might make patients sick. After visiting people, the animals usually take a bath. Their handlers don't want them to carry germs or get sick.

Q Do other animals, like cats and guinea pigs, need baths after their visits too?

Therapy animals need baths after visiting sick people.

A Yes! This is one reason cats aren't used as often in therapy. Most dogs enjoy baths. Most cats do not!

This dog's handler told her to lie down so people could pet her.

People Partners

Therapy animals do not work alone. They need a human partner. This partner is called a handler. They work together as a team. Some handlers tell the animal what to do. Murphy's handler told Murphy to wait a little ways away from Megan. Other handlers take animals out of cages and hold them so they can be petted.

Handlers need training, too. Handlers who take dogs to therapy sessions go to workshops or take classes. They learn how to tell their animal to help therapists.

But most importantly, handlers must learn to control their animals. They must keep their animals calm. They might not need training for this.

Q Can my pet work in therapy?

Dolphin handlers learn how to tell these animals what to do.

A Your pet might be able to visit people to cheer them up. But professional therapy dogs need a great deal of training.

Oscar sits with people on their beds. He makes them feel calm.

Amazing Animals

All therapy animals help people. Oscar is a cat who lives at a nursing home. He visits the rooms of older people. Some of these people are very ill. Oscar often sits with people on their beds. Some of these people pet Oscar. Others just rest with him. Just being around Oscar makes these people feel happier.

Bonner is a huge, fluffy, black Newfoundland. He visits kids at the Children's Hospital in Los Angeles, California. Some of these kids are too sick to leave their hospital rooms. They are bored and lonely. So Bonner visits them. The kids are happy to see him. They pet him and play with him.

Like Bonner, this big, fluffy dog cheers up sick kids.

Koyla is a Great Pyrenees dog like this one.

A woman lies in a hospital bed. She is getting better after having heart surgery. She hasn't opened her eyes in days. Kolya can help. The big, fluffy, white dog climbs up on the woman's bed. He snuggles up next to her. In a few minutes, the woman's eyes flutter open. Therapy animals like Kolya do amazing things every day. They help make people feel better.

Glossary

autism A condition that makes it harder to communicate with people. People with autism might have trouble making friends or being around other people.

cerebral palsy A disease that makes it difficult to control your muscles.

disability A condition that makes doing everyday things harder, such as not being able to see well or walk well.

handler A person who owns and works with a therapy dog.

obedience Being well-behaved; obedience training for animals includes learning to sit, come, and heel.

therapist A person who helps people get treatment for an illness, injury, or disability.

therapy Treatment for an illness or disability.

walker A tool that helps people walk.

Read More

Bozzo, Linda. *Therapy Dog Heroes.* Berkeley Heights, NJ: Bailey Books: 2010.

Hutmacher, Kimberly. *Therapy Dogs.* Mankato, Minn.: Capstone Press: 2010.

Websites

Dolphin-Assisted Therapy
http://www.dolphinassistedtherapy.com

Pet Partners, formerly the Delta Society
www.deltasociety.org

Therapy Dogs International
http://www.tdi-dog.org/

Index

bathing 18, 19
birds 13
Bonner 26
cats 13, 14, 18, 19, 25
cerebral palsy 5
dogs 5, 6, 7, 9, 10, 13, 14, 16, 17, 19, 22, 23, 26, 29
dolphins 13
guinea pigs 13, 18
handlers 17, 18, 21, 22
horses 9, 12, 13
hospitals 9, 10, 17, 26, 29
Koyla 29
Murphy 5, 6, 7, 9, 13, 17, 21
nursing homes 9, 13, 25
Oscar 25
rabbits 13, 14
therapy 5, 6, 9, 13, 22
training 14, 16, 17, 22, 23

About the Author

Connie Colwell Miller is a writer, editor, and teacher of writing. She has written over 70 books for young readers. She especially enjoyed writing about animals because she is one. Miller lives in Mankato, Minnesota, with her husband and three children. All three kids are begging for a dog.